A Fifth Word and Nottingham Playhouse co-production

by James Fritz

Lava was first performed at
Nottingham Playhouse on 15 June 2018
It was revived at Soho Theatre, London, on 5 April 2022

LAVA

by James Fritz

Cast
(in alphabetical order)

VICKY	Kacey Ainsworth
RACH	Bethany Antonia
JAMIE	Oli Higginson
VIN	Dan Parr

Creative Team

Co-Directors	Laura Ford and Angharad Jones
Designer	Amy Jane Cook
Lighting Designer	Alexandra Stafford
Sound Designer	Dan Balfour
Video Designer	Louise Rhoades-Brown
Dramaturg	Nic Wass
Casting Director	Christopher Worrall
Production Manager	Jack Boissieux
Stage Manager	Eva Collins Alonso
Producer	Corinne Salisbury

Director's Note

We are so delighted to finally tour *Lava* to audiences across the UK after an inevitable hiatus due to the pandemic. This tour has been booked, cancelled, rebooked, cancelled and rebooked again! Being back in the rehearsal room with *Lava* feels such a privilege, after originally premiering the production in the Neville Studio with Nottingham Playhouse in 2018. Returning now with a brilliant new cast and being reunited with our creative team is a joy and something we're not taking for granted.

Fifth Word commissioned James with support from Derby Theatre back in 2016: after we saw James' play *Four Minutes Twelve Seconds* we knew immediately we needed to work with him! *Lava* has been developed through numerous round-table reads, workshops and research and development days, with James working tirelessly on many drafts.

Although premiering in 2018, the ideas in *Lava* could not feel more relevant. Way back – in the time before – we often joked that the idea of an asteroid hitting North London and changing the way everyone lived their lives was possibly a stretch too far! But we have now collectively experienced things that felt just as implausible before they became reality: the global pandemic, and more recently the ongoing situation in Ukraine. One thing is for sure: the world feels a far less certain place than it did before. The idea that anything is possible, however unlikely it may seem, certainly speaks to us in a new and different way.

At Fifth Word we commission work that tells the stories of people who find themselves on the margins, or struggle to be heard; and with *Lava* this is literally the case. *Lava* tells the story of Vin, a young man who suddenly stops talking and who is struggling to make sense of his feelings in a world that feels out of control. The play directly speaks to themes people may have experienced in recent years including grief, loss, loneliness, isolation and how we begin to come to terms with something that we thought would never happen to us. It asks important questions about how we approach mental health problems and at a time when we talk about masculinity being in crisis, this play feels more pertinent than ever, questioning why some people's grief or sadness can feel like it has more legitimacy than others.

Lava will connect differently with people depending on their own personal experiences but ultimately, we want audiences to go away believing that there is the possibility of hope even in the face of the inexplicable, and that we can find humour in even our darkest moments.

We look forward to welcoming audiences back to the theatre with this beautiful story of healing and reconnection.

Thank you for attending *Lava* and supporting theatre again.
We hope you enjoy the production.

Laura & Angharad
March 2022

Cast

Kacey Ainsworth | Vicky

Kacey's television credits include: *Sliced* (Dave); *Grantchester* (ITV); *Moving On, The Worst Witch, Call the Midwife, Casualty, The Wright Way, M.I High, Tracey Beaker Returns, Rock Chips, Holby Blue, Hotel Babylon, Eastenders* (BBC); *Midsomer Murders* (Bentley Productions).

Theatre includes: *Sweeney Todd* (Liverpool Everyman); *Holes* (Nottingham Playhouse); *Feed the Beast* (Birmingham Rep/New Wolsey Theatre/Stephen Joseph Theatre); *Calendar Girls* (National Theatre tour); *Steel Magnolias* (ATG); *Carrie's War* (Apollo West End); *Attempts on Her Life* (Royal Court); *Sleep With Me* (National Theatre); *Serving It Up* (Bush Theatre) and *Pale Horse* (Royal Court Upstairs).

Film credits include: *Lynne and Lucy* (BBC); *Mother* (Townley Productions); *We The Kings* (Elemo Films); *Hip Hip Hooray* (Lyndsey Miller); *Girl from Rio* (Casanova Pictures); *Topsy Turvey* (Thin Man Films). Kacey won most popular actress at the National Television Awards in (2002).

Bethany Antonia | Rach

Bethany Antonia can currently be seen playing Kayleigh Shaw in the Netflix original series *Stay Close* and as Margot Rivers in the Netflix series *Get Even.* Previous roles include feature films *There's Always Hope* and *Pin Cushion.*

Oli Higginson | Jamie

Oli Higginson trained at the Guildhall School of Music and Drama.

Oli has recently appeared as Fred in *A Christmas Carol* at the Old Vic. Before that, Oli starred in the West End transfer of Southwark Playhouse's critically acclaimed production of *The Last Five Years,* for which he was nominated for a Stage Debut Award and an Offie Award. Other theatre work includes *The Haystack* (Hampstead Theatre); *Maggie & Ted* (Garrick Theatre); and Brutus in *Julius Caesar* for the Sam Wanamaker Festival at SHakespeare's Globe.

Oli will next be seen in Michael Winterbottom's new Sky Atlantic show *This Sceptred Isle* which will be out later this year, and in the second series of *Bridgerton*, reprising his role from the first series. Oli was recently on screens in Emily Mortimer's *The Pursuit of Love* opposite Lily James for BBC.

Dan Parr | Vin

Dan's theatre credits include: *The Big Corner* (Bolton Octagon); *Road* (Royal Court); *The Kitchen Sink* (The New Vic); *Around the World in 80 Days, Hamlet, A Christmas Carol, Europe, Road, Romeo and Juliet, Kes* (Leeds Playhouse); *Weald* (Finborough Theatre); *Hamlet* (Barbican); *Britannia Waves the Rules, Scuttlers, Pages from My Songbook* (Royal Exchange Theatre); *Wanted! Robin Hood* (Library Theatre) and *DNA* (The Lowry Theatre).

Film includes: *2.0 Lucy, The Rise of the Krays, The Fall of the Krays* and *Halcyon Heights.*

Television includes: *Silent Witness*, *The Musketeers*, *Rocket's Island*, *Casualty*, *The Crimson Field*, and *The Village*.

Dan is one of the founders of *Hear the Picture*, an actor-led audio-description company, exploring creative access in theatre.

Creative Team

James Fritz | Playwright

James Fritz is a writer from South London. His other plays include *Four Minutes Twelve Seconds* (Hampstead Theatre/Trafalgar Studios); *Parliament Square* (Royal Exchange Theatre/Bush Theatre); *Ross & Rachel* (Assembly/BAC/59e59 New York); *Start Swimming* (Young Vic); *The Fall* (Southwark Playhouse/National Youth Theatre); *Comment is Free, Eight Point Nine Nine, Death of a Cosmonaut* (BBC Radio 4) and *Skyscraper Lullaby* (Audible).

He has won the Critics' Circle Theatre Award for Most Promising Playwright, the Bruntwood Prize for Playwriting, the Imison and Tinniswood BBC Audio Drama Awards, and an ARIAS Gold award.

Angharad Jones | Co-Director

Angharad joined touring company New Perspectives as Artistic Director and CEO in October 2021. Formerly she co-founded Fifth Word and was joint Artistic Director alongside Laura Ford for 15 years.

Productions for Fifth Word include: *Lava* by James Fritz, *All the Little Lights* by Jane Upton, *Amateur Girl* by Amanda Whittington, *Wreck* by Toby Campion. Further commissioned playwrights include Mufaro Makubika, Sonali Bhattacharyya, Sophie Ellerby, Phoebe Éclair-Powell, Satinder Chohan, Maureen Lennon.

Angharad's directing credits include: *Maryland* script-in-hand reading (New Perspectives), *Lava* by James Fritz (world premiere Nottingham Playhouse 2018, UK tour); *The Fishermen* (Associate Director for New Perspectives, world premiere tour and West End run); *All the Little Lights* (Associate Director, Nottingham Playhouse/UK tour – nominated for Best New Play at the Writers' Guild Awards and for an Off West End Award for Best New Play; joint winner of the George Devine Award); *Bones* (Edinburgh Festival Fringe/Tristan Bates Theatre/UK tour) and *Painkillers* (Edinburgh Festival Fringe & UK tour).

Angharad@newperspectives.co.uk
www.newperspectives.co.uk

Laura Ford | Co-Director

Laura Ford is co-founder and Artistic Director of Fifth Word.

Recent directing credits for Fifth Word include: *Lava* by James Fritz (Associate Director, Nottingham Playhouse, 2018); *All the Little Lights* by Jane Upton (Nottingham Playhouse/UK tour/Arcola Theatre 2017 – nominated for Best New Play by the Writers' Guild Awards and for Off West End Award for Best New Play; Joint Winner of the George Devine Award); *Bones* by Jane Upton (Edinburgh Festival Fringe/Tristan Bates Theatre/UK tour). Semi-staged readings include: *Are We Dead Yet Benny?* by Phoebe Eclair-Powell (Derby Theatre); *Wreck* by Toby Campion (Nottingham Playhouse) and *Still Here* by Ryan Leader (Nottingham Playhouse).

Laura regularly works with writers to help develop new plays through dramaturgy, directing workshops and showcasing work at different stages. Current plays in development with Fifth Word include a new stage adaption of *We Need New Names* by Mufaro Makubika, *Roadblock* by Sonali Bhattacharyya, *Her Majesty's Playground* by Alia Bano and a new commission with Sophie Ellerby.

Amy Jane Cook | Designer
Amy has been working in performance design for over a decade. In this time she has created sets and costumes for shows both in the UK and abroad.

Theatre design work includes: *All My Sons* (Queen's Theatre); *Baskerville* (Mercury); *The Season* (Royal & Derngate/New Wolsey Theatre); *Jellyfish* (National Theatre); *Wave Me Goodbye* (Theatr Clwyd); *The Importance of Being Earnest* (Watermill, Newbury); *You Stupid Darkness!* (Plymouth Drum); *Absurd Person Singular* (Watford Palace); *The Funeral Director* (Southwark Playhouse – nominated for Best Set Designer – Offie Award Nomination); *Thor and Loki* (Assembly Roxy, Edinburgh/ High Tide Festival); *Jellyfish* (Bush – Offie Award Nomination); *Lava* (Nottingham Playhouse); *Anna Karenina, Barbarians* (Guildhall); *Our Blue Heaven, Never Lost at Home* (New Wolsey Theatre); *Not Talking* (Arcola – Offie Award nomination); *The Rise and Fall of Little Voice* (Theatr Clwyd); *To Dream Again* (Polka Theatre); *Insignificance* (Theatr Clwyd); *Insignificance* (Langham, New York).

Alexandra Stafford | Lighting Designer
Recent theatre credits include: *Mugabe, My Dad and Me* (ETT & Brixton House); *Into Battle* (In Soft Wings Productions); *Cinderella, Bubble, Skellig, Kindertransport* (Nottingham Playhouse); *Around the World in 80 Days* (USA & UK tour New Vic production in partnership with Kenny Wax Family Entertainment); *The Wind in the Willows* (Derby Theatre); *Oh, No George!* (Can't Sit Still); *Babe, The Sheep Pig* (Mercury Theatre Colchester); *All the Little Lights*, (Fifth Word Theatre); *Playhouse Creatures* (The New Vic); *A Thing Mislaid* (Maison Foo); *Aidy the Awesome* (The Gramophones); *Cinderella, Sherlock Holmes & The Hound of the Baskervilles, Betrayal* (York Theatre Royal); *Hard Times* (Oldham Coliseum); *Outsiders, Antigone* (Pilot Theatre); *The Red Tree, Mirror Mirror, Emil & the Detectives* (Red Earth Theatre); *Harvest, Finding Nana* (New Perspectives); *A Tender Thing, The Kreutzer Sonata* (Chipping Norton Theatre) and fourteen pantomimes for Harrogate Theatre.

Dan Balfour | Sound Designer
Dan is a London-based sound designer. He was a nominated for an Off West End, Best Sound Design Award for his work on *Operation Mincemeat* (New Diorama); *Great Apes* (Arcola) and *Blood Wedding* (Omnibus). Dan is the Company Sound Designer for the British-Romanian theatre company, Bezna Theatre.

Credits include: *Lava* (UK Tour); *Tempest* (Pleasance Theatre); *Private Peaceful* (Nottingham Playhouse, UK tour); *The Hatchling* (large scale event, Trigger Productions); *Idyll* (Pentabus Theatre, tour); *Two Character Play* (Hampstead Theatre); *Can I Live, Voices of the Earth* (Complicité); *Beauty and the Beast* (Oxford Playhouse); *Fahrenheit 451* (RCSSD); *The Sugar Syndrome* (Orange Tree); *Pavilion* (Theatre Clwyd); *HOME* (Young Vic); *Counting Sheep* (Belarus Free Theatre); *hang* (Sheffield Crucible); *Wilderness* (Hampstead Theatre); *Operation Mincemeat* (New Diorama Theatre/Southwark Playhouse); *Lava* (Nottingham Playhouse); *Effigies of Wickedness* (Gate Theatre); *Great Apes* (Arcola Theatre) and *VINOVAT, -Ă* (Teatru Replica, Bucharest).

Louise Rhoades-Brown | Video Designer
Louise is a highly skilled video & projection designer specialising in video for theatre and live events. She trained in Motion Graphic Design at Ravensbourne College. Her work can be seen across the UK and internationally.

Theatre and live event credits include: *Young Frankenstein* (English Theatre Frankfurt); *Adam Lambert* (Las Vegas RCM); *Baskerville* (The Mercury); *Stardust* (Roundhouse);

Dick and Angel, Dare to Do It (UK tour); *Macbeth* (UK tour, Watermill Theatre); *Bastille* (Summer Festival tour, RCM); *Zara Larsson* (Spring tour); *One Flew Over The Cuckoo's Nest* (English Theatre Frankfurt); *D-Day75* (Greenham Trust); *The Phlebotomist* (Hampstead Theatre); *Macbeth* (Watermill Theatre, Newbury); *Trial by Laughter* (Watermill Theatre, Newbury, tour); *An Adventure* (Bush Theatre); *Neil Oliver* (UK tour); *It Happened in Key West* (Charing Cross Theatre); *Sweet Charity* (Watermill Theatre, Newbury); *Lava* (Nottingham Playhouse); *Friendly Fires* (Brixton Academy, Animator, RCM); *Br'er Cotton* (Theatre503); *Rothschild & Sons* (Park Theatre, London); *Bananarama* (UK tour, RCM); *Luv Esther* (UK Tour); *Gok Wan, Naked and Baring All* (UK tour); *Legally Blonde* (Korea/Monte Carlo); *Rudimental* (V Festival, RCM); *The Ugly One* (Park Theatre, London); *A Thousand Faces* (Art Sung, Alma Maler, Wilton's Music Hall); *Worst Wedding Ever* (Salisbury Playhouse); *Dracula* (Resorts World, Singapore); *The Island Nation* (Arcola Theatre, London); *Merch Yr Eog* (Theatre Genedlaethol, Cymru); *Bugsy Malone* (Leicester Curve Theatre); *The Trial of Jane Fonda* (The Park Theatre, London); *Box of Photographs* (Polka Theatre); *Legally Blonde* (Leicester Curve Theatre); *Alice's Adventures in Underground* (Animator, Waterloo Vaults); *Chwalfa* (Pontio); *The End of Longing* (Animator, The Playhouse); *The Monster in the Maze* (The Barbican); *Fugee & Wasted* (Southwark Playhouse); *The Merchant of Venice* (Associate, Almeida Theatre); *Gods & Monsters* (Southwark Playhouse); *The Prodigals* (Belgrade Theatre, Coventry); *The Handyman* (UK tour); *Romeo & Juliet* (Headlong, national tour); *The Swallowing Dark* (Theatre503); *Queen with Adam Lambert* (world tour 2014).

www.rhoades-brown.com

Nic Wass | Dramaturg

Nic Wass is Creative Associate at Regent's Park Open Air Theatre and Fifth Word. Nic's roles have included Head of New Work – Maternity Cover (Donmar Warehouse), Associate Dramaturg (RSC), Artistic Associate (Kiln) and deputy to the Literary Manager (Royal Court). Nic is experienced in international writing/translation, working with community groups, circus artists and storytellers, and has mentored writers within the criminal justice system.

Theatre credits include: 2019–2022 seasons (Regent's Park Open Air Theatre); *When This is Over* (Community Project of the Year – Stage Award, Outstanding Drama Initiative - Music and Drama Education awards, Company 3); *Assembly* (Donmar Warehouse); *Mushy: Lyrically Speaking* (Best Stage Production, Asian Media Awards, Rifco); *Lava* (Nottingham Playhouse Studio/Soho Theatre, tour, Fifth Word); *Day of the Living, Myth, Snow in Midsummer* (RSC); *Home Girl, Jinny* (Derby); *The Great Wave* (Catherine Johnson Award, nominated for Most Promising Playwright – Evening Standard), *A Wolf in Snakeskin Shoes, The House That Will Not Stand*, (Olivier Award), *Circles* (co- dramaturg, Catherine Johnson Award), *The Kilburn Passion, The Epic Adventure of Nhamo the Manyika Warrior and His Sexy Wife Chipo, Red Velvet* (Olivier Award) (Kiln); *A Time to Reap* (nominated for Most Promising Playwright – Evening Standard), *Vera Vera Vera* (nominated for Most Promising Playwright – Evening Standard) (Royal Court); *Dream Story* (Gate); *The Big Fellah* (Out of Joint/UK tour).

Christopher Worrall | Casting Director

Christopher is a freelance casting director and has previously worked in-house at The Old Vic and Donmar Warehouse.

Theatre credits as casting director: *The Misfortune of the English, Tom Fool, Two Billion Beats, Last Easter* (Orange Tree Theatre); *Meet Me in St. Louis* (Grange Park Opera); *Missing People* (Leeds Playhouse); *If Not Now When* (National Theatre); *Lava* (Nottingham Playhouse); *Chicken Soup* (Sheffield Crucible).

Theatre credits as Ccasting associate/assistant: *A Very Expensive Poison, All My Sons, The American Clock, A Christmas Carol* (The Old Vic); *Company* (Gielgud Theatre); *Measure for Measure, Aristocrats, The Prime of Miss Jean Brodie, The Way of the World, The York Realist, Belleville, The Lady from the Sea, Committee* (Donmar Warehouse).

Film and TV Credits as casting associate: *Emma, Call the Midwife.*

NOTTINGHAM PLAYHOUSE

Nottingham Playhouse is dedicated to making bold and thrilling theatre in the heart of Nottingham and was named Regional Theatre of the Year in The Stage Awards 2019.

The theatre is a central part of cultural life in Nottingham and, despite the pandemic closing its doors, it proved its ability to adapt and thrive by creating new work and moving to digital platforms where in person audiences have not been possible.

In 2020 its award-winning production of *The Madness of George III* was made available online through NT at Home and it produced its first piece of new digital theatre – an interactive Zoom play for children called *Noah and the Peacock*. Most recently, nearly 29,000 people, including children from 69 schools, watched its online pantomime *Cinderella*. It has continued its commitment to hiring local freelancers who have been hard-hit by the recent crisis, through efforts to produce new work, highlighted in its *Unlocked* festival in autumn 2020, including the world premiere of the recently nominated Broadway World Award production *Bubble* by associate artist James Graham. This commitment continued through *Spring Loaded* in 2021, which included the highly-regarded new digital theatre project *Still Life*.

Recent successes include Mark Gatiss's adaptation of *A Christmas Carol*, which completely sold out and transferred to The Alexandra Palace Theatre for a six-week run, and its 2022 acclaimed production of *Private Peaceful* touring to venues across the country. In summer 2022 its 2013 production of *The Kite Runner* opens on Broadway.

Nottingham Playhouse believes that theatre should be accessible to everyone and offers Pay What You Can evenings, a range of participatory groups for people at risk and has a decades long history of creating work with and for young people.

Nottingham Playhouse Trust Ltd relies on ticket sales for 70% of its income, and continues to fundraise through its Curtain Up appeal. It is a registered charity (no. 1109342).

nottinghamplayhouse.co.uk

Supported using public funding by
ARTS COUNCIL
ENGLAND
LOTTERY FUNDED

Nottingham
City Council

Based in the East Midlands and run by Artistic Director Laura Ford, **Fifth Word** is a leading regional new writing company dedicated to discovering, developing, nurturing and producing the most exciting playwrights of today. We produce urgent, critically-acclaimed new plays that shine a light on under-explored issues and experiences, and tell stories that connect particularly with younger audiences and under-served communities across the UK.

> 'an extraordinary achievement of writer, director and actors... deeply affecting work on a too-urgent subject' *Exeunt Magazine* (on *All the Little Lights*)

We support writers to develop new plays for production and touring. We engage in a thoughtful, rigorous and bespoke process with each playwright we work with. The plays we create amplify stories of those who often go unheard or easily slip through the cracks in society. We aim to shift perspectives, challenge mainstream narratives and foster a love of theatre by harnessing its power for storytelling and human connection.

> 'Observations of the dehumanising influence of the sex industry do not come much sharper' *Guardian* (on *Amateur Girl*)

Previous world premiere productions include WRECK by Toby Campion (Nottingham Playhouse 2017); ALL THE LITTLE LIGHTS by Jane Upton (Nottingham Playhouse/UK tour/Arcola Theatre 2017 – nominated for Best New Play by the Writers' Guild Awards and for OffWestEnd Award for Best New Play; Joint Winner of the George Devine Award); AMATEUR GIRL by Amanda Whittington (UK tour 2014); and BONES by Jane Upton (Edinburgh Festival 2011/UK tour 2012). We have also run numerous flagship engagement projects, working in-depth with different communities in the East Midlands and beyond to empower them to tell their own stories through different artistic mediums. Our most recent community project is LIGHTS UP, which facilitated young women in the East Midlands to interview inspirational female leaders in theatre who came from the region, and to digitally document the work to create a photography exhibition and podcast series (lights-up.fifthword.co.uk).

Fifth Word is a previous winner of the Olwen Wymark Theatre Encouragement Award.

> 'Winning the Encouragement Award for developing new writing, from the Writer's Guild of Great Britain, gave Fifth Word national recognition. Its nurturing of this play is exemplary' *The Stage* (on *Bones*).

Acknowledgements

Fifth Word would like to thank: New Perspectives, Nic Wass, Sarah Brigham, Fiona Buffini, Corinne Salisbury, Adam Penford, Nottingham Playhouse, Derby Theatre, and Nick Hern Books for their ongoing support of the play.

And a special thank you to James Fritz for his incredible talent, patience and perseverance throughout the development of this play.

Fifth Word gratefully acknowledges the support received from: Arts Council England, Nottingham Playhouse and Derby Theatre.

Fifth Word gratefully acknowledges the support received from: Arts Council England, Nottingham Playhouse and Derby Theatre.

Fifth Word Theatre
fifthword.co.uk

LAVA

James Fritz

Acknowledgements

All the actors who helped workshop this play. Nottingham Playhouse for giving it a first home.

Tam for coming up with the title and putting up with mid-rewrite stresses.

Ted, Emma, Fred and Safiyya for bringing these characters so thrillingly into the world.

Nic Wass for her tireless dramaturgy and friendship across a long old process.

And Laura Ford and Angharad Jones, for taking a punt on me all those years ago and putting up with draft after draft after draft after draft with patience, insight and enthusiasm. We've made this together and I couldn't be more excited that it's finally a thing.

J.F.

Well, that was an unexpected interlude.

Thanks to you all, from the bottom of my heart, for keeping the faith through dark times. It's been brilliant being back together.

J.F.
(2022)

Characters

RACH
VIN
VICKY
JAMIE

Note on Text

Silence, for obvious reasons, plays a huge part in this play. I've suggested some places where silence might occur, but trust it throughout. The scenes between Vin and Vicky, in particular, should have painful silences running throughout them.

Dialogue in bold is sent from Vin's phone. It should never be spoken out loud by Vin, but should be able to be read or heard by the audience. I haven't included emoji, x's, etc., but feel free to add as you see fit.

An ellipsis (…) signifies a jump in time.

A line with no full stop at the end indicates an unfinished thought.

A line with a dash at the end indicates an interruption.

This text went to press before the end of rehearsals and so may differ slightly from the play as performed.

STAGE ONE: DENIAL

Time since impact: 15 days 7 hours 4 minutes 12 seconds.

VIN *and* RACH. RACH *is holding a candle.*

RACH   An asteroid

An actual fucking

Asteroid.

I can't be the only one who finds it a bit much.

Silence.

Like

I sort of

Wanna refuse

You know?

Refuse to be part of a world where something that ridiculous can happen.

Silence.

Like, if the news were a TV show, then the moment a little asteroid hit North London and killed twelve thousand people I'd stop watching. I'd be like, 'No thank you, they've gone way too far here.'

You know what I mean? They're taking the mick.

Silence.

What did you think of the vigil? Bit much, weren't it?
My mum's mate. Lucy.
She died.
She lives in London and she was on her way home when it hit.

Silence.

Hence the candle.

She gestures to the candle.

Silence.

Oh my god, you'll love this. I was doing a shift with Becca on Monday

She keeps going round to everyone saying how she almost died

So I was like, 'How did you almost die Becca?'

And she was like, 'I was sposed to go visit my cousin in London that weekend. But I didn't.'
And so I was like, 'So your cousin lives near the impact zone?'
And she was like, 'Not really, why?'

Her cousin lives in Croydon. That's not even London.

Silence.

Where you been hiding Vin?

You just disappeared on me. Came into work and there was a Vin-shaped hole where you used to be.

I text you. I know you've seen them. Did I do something to

How you been anyway? You been up to much?

Brief silence.

Right. You know it's pretty rude not to answer people in the same way it's pretty rude disappearing on your mates without a word. I'm just saying.

VIN *doesn't say anything.*

I get it.

Nice talking to you.

Fucking rude.

...

RACH   Sorry I called you rude.

I went into work and I said I saw Vin he's rude and
Supervisor Ian was like oh yeah he just don't talk
any more. And I was like what d'you mean he don't
talk any more and he was like he just stopped talking
which was a bit of a problem it being a call centre
and all.

That true then?

That's weird innit mate?

Is it like a brain thing?

My grandad had that.
After his stroke.

'Cept his was a bit different
Like
He could talk right
But he could only say one word which was

'Judy'

You know, like the name? I mean, he'd use it for
everything.

We'd be like
You hungry Grandad?
And he'd say 'Judy.'
You warm enough?
'Judy!'

And we were like, 'Who the fuck is Judy?' you
know, because my nan's name's not Judy my nan's
name's Jane.
And Nan was all like, 'Oh he probably picked it up
off the telly.'
But then

At his funeral
This woman shows up
Looking all
You know

Really glam right
And she don't say nothing
But she leaves some flowers
And on the card it says
'Forever yours. Judy.'

So what d'you think that was all about then?!

Can you write things down? Or your phone. You
could text? You can't use your phone? I'm sorry
mate. That is rough.

People don't just stop talking for no reason. Do they?

You want me to leave you alone?

Alright then I'll leave you alone.

...

RACH *and* VIN. VIN*'s front door.*

RACH   I've decided.

I'm not going to leave you alone. Ian gave me your
address which is probably illegal but then we both
know he's not great at his job is he?

Look how annoyed he is! He won't even look at me.

Vin!
Oi Vin!

VIN *refuses to look at her.*

Vin!
Vin!
Vin!
Vin!
Vin!
Vin!
Vin!
Vin!

I'm just gonna keep saying your name until you look
at me.

Vincent!
Vinno!
Vin!
Vin!
Vinny!
Vin.
Vin
Vin.
Vin.
Vin.
Vin.
Vin.
Vin.
Viiiiiiiiiiiiiiiiiiiiiiiiiiiiiiiiiiiiiiiiiiiiiiiiiiiiiiiiiiiiiiiiiiiiiiiiiiiiii
iiiiiiiiiiiiiiiiiiiiiiiiiiiiiiiiiiiiiiii

She takes a breath.

Iiiiiiiiiiiiiiiiiiiiiiiiiiiiiiiiiiiiiiiiiiiiiiiiiiiiiiiiiiiiiiiiiiiiiiiiiiiiii
iiiiiiiiiiiiiiiiiiiiiiiiiiiiiiiiiiiiiin.

He looks at her. She grins.

Hiya.

Not being able to talk. Fucking hell.
I wouldn't last an hour. Having all that inside of me
and no place to put it I'd worry I'd explode.
At work. They said you stopped talking round the
same time as the asteroid. Same day, they thought.
That true?

VICKY   (*From inside the house.*)
         Vin?! Who's that?

RACH   That your mum?

         You gonna invite me in?

         Okay.

         Look how 'bout this. Here's my address.
         Knock round any time.

...

VIN *and* VICKY. VIN*'s house.*

VICKY   Hiya love.

Who was at the door?

A friend?

Anyone I know?

Okay.

Still not

That's fine.

There's food if you're

Oh! I forgot to say, that cat was back. I was stood in the garden and there he was, acting like he was the little King of Everything, oh you shoulda seen him.

Seems very friendly. For a cat, anyway.

I don't think he's got an owner, he's got no, whatsit, collar and he doesn't seem very well you know, cared for, his fur's sorta mangy, mind you that's just how some of them look isn't it?

I've given him some food either way, I thought
what's the harm, you know, a bit of food, I picked up
some, whatsit, cat biscuits from the Co-op I thought
maybe I'll keep leaving some out for him, see if he
comes back, what d'you think?

Might be nice. Having him in the house? Eh?

Seems friendly.

I wondered.

Fish and chips.
We haven't done that since

We could watch a film together.

Or football. Is there any good football on?

A film then.

Doesn't have to be fish and chips.

A curry?
Thai?
Chinese?
Pizza?
Barbecue?
Vietnamese?

Or I could cook something.

Or we could go out for dinner.

Or we could
We could

Okay.

I'll choose then, shall I?

...

VIN *is outside* RACH*'s house.*

RACH   Vin.

You're at my house.

Hello.

You want to come in? You can come in but just so you
know it's a bit weird in there at the moment. We just
got back from Lucy's funeral and Mum's a bit

They've only just been able to have it. Her son
Jamie. He gave this amazing speech and everyone
was a wreck.

Kinda strange knowing someone who was in it.
You know what I mean?

D'you know what? It's pretty depressing in there.
D'you wanna go somewhere and get some cans?

...

They drink cans overlooking the town.

RACH   There's something going on round here.

Things keep disappearing.

Have you noticed? Like someone's stealing them.

It started small. Little things so you wouldn't.
The post box by my house. Gone. A lamp post on
Tudor Road I swear I passed it every day and then
one day. Gone.

Then it was The Black Sheep. Loved that pub. Then
the swimming pool just vanished and nobody talked
about it. A whole fucking swimming pool. Water and
everything. And it wasn't like it was demolished
there'd be bricks and stuff. It was just like one day it
was there and the next day it wasn't. Same thing
happened to the library. Remember the old library?

VIN *shakes his head.*

No course you don't. No one does. That's part of it
you see. These things vanish and then everyone acts
like they were never there to begin with.

Not me though. I pay attention. I'm on to them.
The thieves. Maybe it's aliens. Eh? Don't look at me
like that. If an asteroid's acceptable then I don't see
how aliens is pushing things too far.

Or maybe we're like in a simulation or a game and
we're just being deleted pixel by pixel. There's got to
be an explanation.

Maybe that's where your voice has gone. Same place
as the swimming pool.

Let's hope not. Eh?

VIN *nods.*

I wondered if you wanted if you fancied that maybe
we could work it out together. I could help you try
and get it back. If you wanted.

Because. Well. You know, and I don't know if this makes any, but I thought I'd

Cos when you did used to speak at work or in the pub I always kinda liked the things you had to say.

And I miss hearing them, if I'm honest.

VIN *smiles*.

Eurgh, that was fucking embarrassing.

What is it about having to fill a silence that makes some people say
Like
The most embarrassing shit

Forget I ever

I want to help
Is what I'm trying to say.

I'm here if you need me.

Silence.

I don't know if I should

You see Supervisor Ian at work told me something.

He told me something and I wasn't sure if I should say but.

He told me he heard that your dad died in London.

Is that true?

He told me your dad died and you haven't been able to talk to anyone since.

Because that makes sense.

That makes sense I bet.

A moment.

VIN *nods*.

Oh mate.

I am so sorry.

...

VIN *and* VICKY. VIN*'s house.*

VICKY   He's gonna be okay.

That's what the vet said.

Just a bit undernourished.

Wasn't sure if that was the right thing to
Taking him to the vet's.

I mean he might have another owner but he seemed
a bit

He's made himself at home here so it's only fair we
take care of him. Don't you think?

As I was leaving I bumped into Will Paxton with his
Labrador. He likes you.

Said that job offer's still going if you want it. So that's
good isn't it?

What do you think?

Might be good for you. Get out of the house. Get you
off that sofa.

Silence.

Bit of exercise. Lots of lads your age working on his
site he says. So that might be

But you know a job like that. You can't do the silent
act. Health and safety. Not safe for the other lads.
You know?

So I thought maybe together we could look at some
things. Websites or. Get you talking again. Because I

know things have been a bit rough, and we've all got
our own ways of

But we've got to get on with it, haven't we?
That's all we can do. Really.

So I'll tell him yes?

Yes?

Okay.

Good.

Good lad.

Vin's alright I told him. My Vin's doing alright.

What shall we call him then?

The cat.

Any suggestions?

                          ...

Outside RACH*'s house.*

RACH   Vin.

          You're at my house again. We really need to sort out
          a system.

          I had fun the other night.

          Listen there's something I should

          JAMIE *enters from the house.*

JAMIE   Rach?
          You ready?

RACH   Oh.

Vin this is Jamie. He's staying with us.

JAMIE   Hey man.

RACH   Just for a little while.

JAMIE   How's it going?

RACH   Vin can't talk.

JAMIE   What like, at all?
HOW'S IT GOING MATE?

RACH   You don't need to shout.

JAMIE   Right.

RACH   Jamie's from London. He was in the

JAMIE   Impact Event.

RACH   You remember I told you about his mum.

JAMIE   She died. Yeah.

RACH   His house might have structural damage so he's
gonna stay with us until it's sorted.

Is it alright if I tell him. Vin?

RACH   Vin's dad died in London too.

JAMIE   You're kidding?

JAMIE *hugs* VIN *unexpectedly and fervently.*

It is so nice to meet you mate.

RACH   I was gonna take Jamie to The Talbot. For a pint.

Why don't you come?

STAGE TWO: ANGER

Residents displaced: 132,157.

VIN, RACH *and* JAMIE. *The pub*.

JAMIE   Are you furious Vin?

           I'm still fucking furious.

           It's a dereliction of duty.

RACH   You said.

JAMIE   A dereliction of duty.
           Someone must have seen it coming.
           I don't care what they say. The billions they spend
           on satellites.
           Weather technology.
           And NASA. What were they doing? Having a fag?

RACH   It does seem a bit mad.

JAMIE   My dad thinks we should sue them.

RACH   Who / NASA?

JAMIE   She died in my arms Vin, did you tell him Rach?

RACH   No I –

JAMIE   One minute she's there and the next

RACH   You don't have to talk about it if you don't feel –

JAMIE   No it's fine.
           Honestly.
           It helps actually.
           The thing I can't get over. It's the randomness.

           The chances of it hitting Earth in the infinity of space.
           The chances of it hitting London.

           And then the chances that my mum would be cycling
           through at that exact moment. That exact moment,
           not five minutes before, or five minutes after.

What about your dad? Did he live round there?

VIN *shakes his head*.

RACH   Vin's dad's from here.

JAMIE   So he was just visiting?

VIN *nods his head*.

Oh mate. At least my mum, you know, she passed through there every day.

My house is only just outside the impact zone. We still can't go back. Structural damage.

RACH   I told him.

JAMIE   They rehoused us in this shitty B&B in Basingstoke, you ever been to Basingstoke?

VIN *shakes his head*.

Don't bother.

RACH   Why didn't your dad come too?

JAMIE   It is so funny being back round here. It's like stepping back in time.

Hasn't changed since I was a kid.
Used to come here all the time Vin.

RACH   We're sort of like cousins.

JAMIE   I'd say more like mates. When we were kids.
How do you two

RACH   We worked together.
Call centre.

JAMIE   Oh that is so interesting.

RACH   Okay.

JAMIE   Sometimes
And you'll love this
Sometimes when call centres ring me up I pretend that

I'm really interested I sort of string them along for
ages and pretend I'm going to give loads of money
and then right at the last minute I'll do like a silly
voice or something and tell them it was all a wind-up.

RACH   Yeah.
          We love it when people do that.

JAMIE   Can I ask
          I don't want to sound rude but
          How can you work in a call centre when you can't,
          you know…

RACH   Vin doesn't work there any more. He used to speak.

          It's only been since his dad

JAMIE   Oh mate.
          You know that makes perfect sense to me. Going
          through something like this. It takes a physical toll.

          Was he killed by the initial impact? Or in the
          aftermath?

          Do you know exactly where he was?

RACH   Maybe we should talk about something else.

JAMIE   Did you have trouble organising the funeral?
          We had terrible trouble. The backlog.

RACH   You even had a funeral yet?

          VIN *shakes his head*.

JAMIE   Ours took forever to get it sorted.
          Great day though
          Right Rach?
          Like, sad, but.
          A celebration as well.

          We did all these things
          Like we got my mate to DJ
          And we asked everyone to wear like their craziest
          colours.

One of my uncles insisted on wearing black.
And I was like
Come on man
It's not what she would've wanted.

RACH   I thought your speech was nice.

JAMIE   Thank you. That is so

It was like
The hardest thing I've ever had to write
But also
In a way
The easiest.

I'd be happy for you to read it, Vin. You know, if you
thought it might help.

A moment. VIN *nods.*

You know what. I've got a copy somewhere –

RACH   You don't have to

JAMIE   I don't mind.

He looks for the speech on his phone.

There you are.

You don't have to read it now.

Well you can read it now if you want to I don't mind.

VIN *starts to read the speech.*

JAMIE *watches him. It takes a while. Eventually*
VIN *passes back the phone.*

There's actually another page if you want to

JAMIE *flicks the page over.*

VIN *carries on reading.*

VIN *'s finished the speech. Hands back the phone.*

JAMIE   Thanks man.

Hope that was helpful.

A moment. VIN *nods.*

...

VIN *and* RACH.

RACH   I'm sorry about him.

I know he can be a bit

Mum and Dad didn't tell me he was coming. He just showed up and they were like Jamie's coming to stay with us for a while be nice to him he's been through a lot.

Still. Might be nice? Having someone else who knows what you're going through?

Suddenly VIN *texts her. We can see what he says.*

VIN   **Rach.**

RACH   Oh my god. You text me.

VIN   **Yeah.**

RACH   You did it again!

How long have you been able to text me?

That's great Vin. That's got to be a step in the right direction don't you think?

VIN   **I need to tell you**

RACH   Okay.

VIN   **There's been a mix-up**

RACH   What about?

VIN   **Dad didn't die in London.**

RACH   What.
          What are you talking about?

VIN   **Work assumed**

RACH   Why would you let me think that?

VIN   **I'm sorry. I came round to tell you the truth. But Jamie**

RACH   What truth?

Whatever's going on. You can tell me.

VIN   **He didn't die in London. He died the same day.**

...

VIN, RACH *and* JAMIE.

JAMIE   The same day?

RACH   Vin found him on the kitchen floor.

JAMIE   Oh mate. You could've told me.

RACH   He felt embarrassed.

JAMIE   Well.
He shouldn't. Grief's grief, you know.
It doesn't matter if it's from an asteroid or a car accident or what did you say?

RACH   A heart attack.

JAMIE   It all counts.

If anything it's easier for me knowing twelve thousand other families are going through the same thing, you know what I mean?

RACH   He's sorry he misled you.

JAMIE   No apology necessary.

And my offer still stands. If ever you want someone to talk to.

We could go for a pint or a walk?

RACH   What do you think Vin?

JAMIE   Another time maybe.

I'll stop pestering you.

How's your mum coping with things?

...

VIN *and* VICKY. VIN's *house*.

VICKY   Gus.

That's the name I've chosen.

Short for Augustus.
What do you think?
Do you think he looks like a Gus?

I do.

Gus.

Gus.

I like it.

So come on then. How's the new job going?
Will treating you alright? Yeah.

That's so good Vin. That's so good. I mean it.

I'm really proud of you.
Working.
I know it must be hard.

Sarah said she saw you.
In the pub. With a girl. Was it that one that came to
the house?

I think that's. Great.

Really.

I think it's wonderful that you feel comfortable
enough to.

That there's someone you can.

I'd love to meet her.

Why don't you bring her round, eh?

Or not.

Up to you.

...

VIN *and* RACH.

RACH   Jamie's mum's gonna have her name on a wall.
          That's mad innit?

          I gotta ask

VIN   **What?**

RACH   Does it piss you off that your dad died the same day
          as like, the maddest natural disaster in our lifetime?

          I mean it's pretty unlucky.

VIN   **come on.**

          don't ask me that.

RACH   Why not?

          Now you can text me I can finally ask you questions
          that don't end in yes or no

          And what, you think I'm gonna waste that asking
          what you had for breakfast or whether or not you got
          off with Maria at the staff party which everyone
          knows you did by the way –

          He smiles. Shrugs.

          Does it piss you off that he died the same day?

          You can be honest.
          It'd piss me off.

VIN   **Honestly?**

          A moment. Then –

          Yeah
          It's fuckin annoying

RACH   I knew it. It makes you feel –

VIN   **Insignificant.**
          Invisible.

          like why that day

RACH Right?

VIN **Why THAT EXACT FUCKIN DAY**
FUCKSAKE

  A moment.

  Sometimes
  I'm reading about it
  and I'm like
  fuck them
  And their memorials

  A moment.

  And then
  You know
  I feel like a dick.

RACH No.
  That's normal.
  I'd feel the same.
  Honest.

  The not talking. Is it like you don't want to talk, so
  you don't? Or you try and talk but you can't?
  I've heard you talk before. You were pretty good at it.

VIN **The words are in there.**
  But it's like they're in a lift
  And it gets stuck halfway up

RACH Right. That makes sense.

VIN **Speaking now would feel**

  Impossible.

RACH Do you think you'll ever be able to talk to anyone?

VIN **To anyone?**

RACH To me.

  Silence.

  Don't hate me.

But I've been looking it up. And there are things you can do. To help.

Like there's an exercise where you hum quietly to yourself every morning. Get used to the feeling of your voice in your throat again. Just a little mmmmmmmmmm.

You know. Maybe you could start doi–

VIN *shakes his head*.

I just thought it might help. Or there's this other article I read –

What's the matter?

VIN   **I don't need you to help me.**

RACH   Okay.

Well. Okay.

VIN   **I didn't btw**

RACH   Didn't what?

VIN   **Get off with Maria.**

...

VIN *and* VICKY. VIN*'s house*.

VICKY   Good day at work love?

Will treating you alright?

VIN *nods*.

That's good. That's really good.
And the other lads. Been making some friends?

VIN *shrugs*.

Only I saw Will and he says you never came in.
Says he hasn't seen you down at the site once.

Where have you been going?

Come back here. Come back.

I just want to know what you've been doing. Because my mind's been racing love, it has. Because as far as I'm concerned you've been leaving this house and going to work and in actuality you've been going off to god knows where.

Are you in trouble? Is there something you need to tell me?

He shakes his head.

God. Sometimes you can be so

Look, Vincent. If you don't want to work there just say. It was just a suggestion. You don't have to lie to me.

I'm only trying to help. I just thought that it might

Because sitting round here all day isn't gonna make you feel any better is it? Is it?

'No Mum it isn't.' 'Sorry Mum thanks for trying.'

I mean, you're not a kid any more, you've got to try something? Surely? Snap yourself out of it somehow?

No.

Okay.

Let's just

···

VIN *and* RACH. RACH*'s bedroom.*

RACH   There's nothing there now, I'm telling you. A third of Tunnel Road just gone. I used to walk that way to work, it's fucking annoying.

It goes up to number 32 and then it just stops. I asked
this old guy who lived there what happened to the
other houses and he looked at me like I was mad and
just said, 'It always stopped at number 32.' I was
like, are you on a wind-up! The swimming pool was
bad enough. But this!

What was his name. Your dad. You've never told me?

VIN   **Horatio**

RACH   Really?

VIN   **No.**

RACH   Dickhead.

VIN   **Phil.**

RACH   Phil.

         The other day, when I asked, you said you hadn't had
         his funeral yet.

VIN   **Mum didn't want one.**

RACH   She didn't want one?

VIN   **Didn't see the point.**

         Brief silence.

RACH   What did he do, your dad?

VIN   **Electrician.**

RACH   Was he any good?

VIN   **He was**
         Fucking awful

RACH   Come on.

VIN   **Seriously. The worst.**

         When I was four
         He rewired my bedside lamp.
         Electrocuted me.

RACH   No.

VIN   **Flew across the room.**
       See that.

       He shows her a burn.

       Man was a liability.

RACH   You must miss him.

       Silence.

       How's your mum?

       She still pissed off about the job?

VIN   **I tried.**
       Went down there.
       But couldn't.

RACH   You gonna try again?

VIN   **No point.**

RACH   Maybe there's a job we can think of where being
       silent's a good thing.

       Like a guard at Buckingham Palace. Or a librarian.

       You'd make a good accomplice. You know. To a crime.
       You could be like the driver or something and when
       the police interrogate you asking like where are they
       where are your partners you'll be like

       Ooh. You could be a lip-sync artist?

       Don't look at me like that.

       It's a thing. I'll show you a clip

                        ...

RACH *is lip syncing to a famous song. She is quite good.*
VIN *starts to enjoy it.*

She encourages him to join in. He refuses.

She gets to the climax of the song. They dance and it is silly.

There's a moment. They stare at each other.

Brief silence.

RACH   Vin.

            Am.
            Am I the only person you can text?

VIN   **Course**

RACH   'Course'. I don't know do I.

            Just me. No one else?

            VIN *shakes head.*

            Why?

            What's special about me, I mean?

            Must be something.

            A moment between them.

            They almost kiss.

            VIN *moves away.*

            Sorry.

            No.

            I'm a

            Sorry. I shouldn't have done that. I thought maybe.

            I don't know what I thought.

STAGE THREE: BARGAINING

Total raised for survivors: £2,751,570.

VIN's house.

VICKY   I think I'm going a bit mad.

This morning the neighbour you know the bin Nazi she caught me out on the street having a full-blown conversation with the cat. In my nightie.

He was out there and it was raining and I was worried about him being near the road. And I kept saying

'Gus if you come in I'll give you some smoked salmon.'
'Gus if you come in I'll let you sleep on the bed tonight.'

And the neighbour she looked at me like 'what is that madwoman doing?' And so I waved at her. But she didn't wave back.

So that's the last time I can show my face out the front door, eh?

How was last night then? You have a good time?

Can't wait to meet her. Your mysterious pub friend.

Do you
Do you talk to her Vin? You know. Out loud.

A moment.

VIN *shakes his head*.

Okay.

So there really isn't anyone who you

He shakes his head.

Well. Just so I. Just so I know.

…

VIN *and* RACH.

RACH   The other night.

VIN   **There's something
        I should say.**

RACH   No
        You don't have to.
        I feel awful.
        Feel like a right dickhead

VIN   **No.**

RACH   There's you
        And you're grieving
        You're in grief
        And you're telling me all this stuff about your grief
        and your dad and
        And there's me
        And I'm just just launching myself at you like a
        I don't know
        A sex pest or
        A

        And
        And now you're laughing.
        You're laughing at me. That's nice. That's making
        me feel less embarrassed thanks.

VIN   **It's alright.**

RACH   No.
        It was stupid.

I'm sorry.

You don't have to worry.
It won't happen again.

Brief silence.

VIN   **How's Jamie?**

RACH   I thought he'd've gone home by now. I don't even
         know what he's still doing here.
         His dad's in Basingstoke.

         Mum's still in overdrive. Fresh towels. Clean sheets.
         Orange juice.

         He's starting to annoy me a bit. If I'm honest.

         Is that bad?

         I know he's been through a lot but.

         He drops references to it all the time.

         Like, all the time.

         I'll be like. 'Pass the butter.' And then he goes all sad
         and is like 'Oh. My mum used to love butter.'

         I'm gonna take him to the pub.

         Mum's making me.

         You wanna come?

         Please come.

                              ...

VIN, RACH *and* JAMIE. *The pub.*

JAMIE   My mum would've loved this pub.
         She'd have been like, this pub. It's got such a weird
         crowd. I love it.

RACH   It's not that weird.

JAMIE   It is.
         Come on.
         In a good way. Don't you think?

Like, who's that guy in the old England shirt who's
talking to himself outside?

RACH   David Beckham?
That's what we call him.

JAMIE   Hilarious. He is mad.

RACH   Yeah.

JAMIE   Like an actual madman.

RACH   Story goes he came home from watching England
Argentina in the pub to find out his whole family had
died in a fire. Wife. Two little girls. He hasn't taken
off the shirt since.

Could be bollocks.

JAMIE   Right.

Silence.

You know when I told the barman I was a London
survivor he gave me a free shot. I get that sort of
reaction all the time.

I've just felt so welcome since I got here.

I hope I haven't been too annoying.
Just this random guy from your childhood showing
up at your house uninvited and bumming everyone
out by mentioning his dead mum all the time.

RACH   Why would you think that?

JAMIE   Because I really appreciate it. I do.

It's just what I need being round here.

You know. There's nothing going on.

In a good way.

I was gonna ask.
Since I'm staying.

Do you think there are any jobs going?

At the call centre?

RACH   You wanna work with me? Why?

JAMIE   Might as well keep myself busy.

RACH   You won't enjoy it.

JAMIE   Meet some new people.

RACH   Vin tell him he won't enjoy it.

JAMIE   It can't be that bad.

RACH   It is.

JAMIE   Then why would anyone work there?

RACH   Because they need money.

Silence.

It's not forever

JAMIE   No

RACH   I got a plan.

JAMIE   That's great.

RACH   Save enough.
Move out.
Start my own business

JAMIE   What business?

RACH   Don't matter.
So long as it does well. Which it will.

And then once that's up and running and everyone knows who I am

You'll laugh.

JAMIE   I won't.
I promise.

RACH   I'm gonna run for Mayor.

JAMIE   What like with the gold chains?

RACH   I told you not to laugh.

JAMIE   I'm not. Sorry.

RACH   This town is the best.
        It is.
        It's fucking amazing.
        Just needs a bit of fixing.

        Most at my college would give me that same look.
        Couldn't wait to get away.
        Even those that knew they weren't going anywhere
        spent their whole time putting it down.

        I'm like well do something about it. Make it better.
        Don't just fuck off and leave it to die.

        So that's my plan. Start a shit-hot local business.
        Run for Mayor. Sort shit out.

JAMIE   Well. I'd vote for you.

RACH   Don't take the piss.

JAMIE   I'm serious.
        I think that's great. I think you'd be great.

        Don't you Vin?

        VIN *nods*.

RACH   I can ask.
        At work.
        I'm sure they'll take you.
        But

        Trust me. You'll hate it.

                            ...

JAMIE   I love it!
        What a job. Seriously.

        At first I was like, this is really boring all you do is
        sit there and call people.
        And then I was like, wow. This is really cool. All you
        do is sit there and call people. Talk to them, you
        know. Conversations.

I've had so many interesting conversations today you know people can be so fascinating if you let them. There was this one lady who was eighty-four and she told me her life story.

RACH   They'll do that.
        You've got to be firm.

JAMIE   No no it was amazing.

        She told me the most impossible thing.

        She told me that she grew up during the Hungarian revolution.
        And when she was twenty-one she fell in love
        With a man called Victor.
        But one day, about a week before her wedding,
        Victor was shot dead. Right in front of her.

        Her heart was broken. She swore off romance forever.
        Cut to, she's in her fifties and she's still all alone
        And she's walking her dog in the park when she
        bumps into this man and she looks up and she
        realises. It's him. It's Victor.

RACH   Shut up.

JAMIE   Her great love.
        In the flesh. Only older.
        And of course she thinks she's seen a ghost
        That he's come back to haunt her
        Until she remembers that Victor had a

        Twin brother

        Who she'd never met.

RACH   Fuck off!

        You're joking.

JAMIE   I know right? So they reconnected and suddenly she found herself falling in love with the brother and they've been together thirty-two years.

What are the chances of that?

Isn't that like fucking romantic?

RACH   Vin he's such a show-off.
He got like ten donations on his first day.

JAMIE   Is that good? I didn't even notice.

Thanks so much for getting me in.

RACH   No worries.

It was actually nice having someone to talk to.

JAMIE *winces*.

Your thumb playing up?

JAMIE   It's no big deal.

RACH   He dislocated it Vin.

JAMIE   I dislocated it Vin.

RACH   It was during the

JAMIE   During the impact yeah that's right.

We were running for our lives and this girl she
tripped and I hauled her up and as I did

Didn't want to leave anyone behind you know.

It was fine. Just meant I couldn't practice guitar for a
few weeks, that's all.

RACH   My dad's got a guitar.
I'm sure he'd let you have a go.

JAMIE   Oh god no, I'm too shy.

…

RACH's *house.* JAMIE *is holding a guitar.*

JAMIE   So I've been playing for a little while.
Just sort of messing about.

He plays a supercool riff.

You know. Just sort of.

He plays another supercool riff. Maybe sings a note.

So yeah.
I'm just sort of –

*Without missing a beat he launches into a sad,
beautiful, sincere, slightly irritating song. He sings
every verse and every chorus. Every time* VIN *thinks
he's going to stop he keeps going, seemingly forever.
Eventually, after an eternity, the song finishes.*
RACH *claps.* VIN *does one or two claps.*

RACH   That was.
         Yeah.

JAMIE   Thanks yeah. I played it at Mum's funeral. Every
         time I sing it it's like she's singing it with me.

         Silence.

         Did your dad have a favourite song Vin?

         VIN *shakes his head.*

         There's also this one.

         *He starts the first few bars of another very sincere,
         probably irritating song.*

                          ...

VIN *and* VICKY. VIN*'s house.*

VICKY *about to leave.* VIN *on the couch.*

VICKY   Okay then.

         I'm off out.

         There's a pizza in the fridge and I've already given
         Gus his food so don't give him any more you know
         what he's like.

What you doing with yourself?

You seeing your mates tonight?

He shrugs.

Okay.

Can I ask

I've seen, Vin.

I've

I've noticed that

You text her. A lot.

You feel alright texting her?

A moment. VIN *nods.*

Well.
That's good, isn't it?
That's great.

That's a good step, eh?

I wonder I've been wondering

maybe.

Maybe you could try texting

me?

VIN *freezes.*

It could be good for us. A good step for us. You could start telling me what you want. Answering my questions. We could text. Or I could talk and you could text.

What do you say? Shall we give it a go?

VIN *shakes his head.*

No.

Okay.

Am I

Am I doing something wrong, love? Because if I am just tell me and I'll try and stop I will

VIN *shakes his head*.

Okay. Well. Let me know.

I won't be late.

...

VIN *and* RACH.

RACH   I'm getting used to having him around.

It's nice having a friend at work again.

Everyone fucking loves him. It's annoying.

The other day I came into the break room and Jamie was sat there with everyone looking at him. Turns out he's been telling the story of how his mum died because everyone had this like devastated look on their faces.

Even Supervisor Ian looked like he'd been crying. I know.

Still think it's weird that Jamie seems so sort of. Fine. You know what I mean? After everything he's been through.

I mean the things he must have seen that day.

And his mum. God knows what he's feeling.

VIN *nods*.

Idiot. Course you know.

VIN   **It's okay.**

RACH   No. Vin. I'm sorry.

I thought
And this is just an idea
But
We could have like a funeral for your dad.
Or not a proper funeral.
It wouldn't have to be formal or anything.
We could go to the park.
Light a fire.
Drink some cans.
Just something to mark his life.
You know?
Maybe that's
It might be the reason that you can't
That you're finding it hard to talk about him.

Because if you've had no release

VIN   **Nah.**

Thanks.

RACH   Okay.

It was just a suggestion.

Well

What about talking to Jamie?

He offered

And he's obviously dealing with losing his mum

Differently. To you.

He might be able to give you some advice?

It's worth a try isn't it?

For me?

...

JAMIE *and* VIN.

JAMIE   Mate.

I am so glad you wanted to do this.

Seriously. You'll be helping me as much as I help you.

So.

Before we start.

I wanted to ask you. It's a bit. You know.

Is. Is anything going on between you and Rach?

Because she's fucking great you know. She's really helping me get through this. Well, you know.

And I wouldn't want to do anything about it if I was stepping on any toes. Or. Getting in the way of anything. So

Brief silence.

Cool. I didn't think so.

So.

Rach said you wanted to talk a bit about how I deal with what's happened.

I don't know how much help I can be.

If you're anything like me you're in this place where you're like 'why, why did this have to happen to me' you know?

One thing that helps me get through the day is that every morning I wake up and I dig deep inside myself and I really interrogate how I'm feeling. You know? What's going on in here. And once I've done that I know what I can do for the rest of the day to keep myself right.

Sometimes it's as simple as going for a walk and thinking yes. Mum might be gone.

But there is still a lot of good in the world. I'm still here. I can still live. Breathe. Enjoy myself. Have a beer.

And

I'm alright. I'm okay.

So. I brought a pen and paper.
I wondered. If you felt comfortable.

Maybe you could start by writing down a few words about how you've been feeling.

VIN *draws something*.

Okay.
So you've drawn a cock and balls.
That's great.
That's really.
That's funny.

Why don't we put the pen and paper away.

···

VIN *and* RACH.

RACH   You think you're a comedian?

       VIN hesitates. Nods.

       She punches him in the arm.

       What's the matter with you?
       He's just being nice.

VIN   **Yeah really nice.**

RACH   He sympathises

VIN   **Jamie's so nice.**

RACH   Why you being a dick?

       Don't you want to get better?

       Silence.

VIN   **Okay.**
         I'll do it.

RACH   Do what?

VIN   **A funeral for Dad.**

RACH   Oh.

         Really? You don't have to.

VIN   **Might be nice.**
         Just me and you?

RACH   If that's what you want.

         Just me and you.

                        ...

VIN *and* RACH. *The park with cans.*

RACH   Okay.

         Don't really know how to

         So. We're here today to celebrate the life of Phil.

         Husband to Vicky.
         Dad to Vin.
         Dodgy electrician from what I hear.

         Phil. Wish I'd met you.

         But I know your son and if he's any reflection on you
         then you must have been a top bloke. You're gone
         too soon.

         This is. This is something Vin text for me to read out.

         'Dad

         I miss you

Sorry for every time I was a dickhead
Every time I annoyed you
Or wasn't what you wanted me to be.

She pauses.

I don't know
How to say
What I need to
But

It feels like a bit of
me has sunk into
The ground
And I don't know how to get it out.

I don't remember
What things were like
When they weren't
Like this
And I wish they could go back.

I love you.

Your son.

Vin.'

Vin. Is that really how you feel?

That was really beautiful. I mean it.

Okay,

Cheers Phil.

They pour out their beer cans.

Shall we do a minute's silence?

Alright then.
Three
Two

They have a minute's silence.

They look at each other.

RACH *watches the last ten seconds*.

Right then.

Pub?

Is it alright if I invite Jamie? He's been having
a tough week.

···

The pub.

JAMIE   I've been having a tough week Vin.

Well you know how it is.

It comes in waves you know.
Some days I almost forget.
And then blam.

I remember.

Brief silence.

RACH   Shall I get the drinks in?

···

One drink in.

RACH   Cheers.
Vin would like to say sorry. About the cock-and-balls
thing. Wouldn't you Vin?

VIN *nods*.

JAMIE   Nothing to say sorry for.

RACH   Here's to your dad Vin.

JAMIE   To your dad.

They drink.

And my mum.

···

Two drinks in.

JAMIE   What d'you mean it's disappearing?

RACH   I mean it's fuckin' disappearing. Cheers.

Vin'll tell you.

The bus stop on Woodland Road. The top three floors of Welstead House. The fucking King Arms vanished last week. Well, half of it anyway –

The other half's still there but who wants to drink in half a pub you know?

JAMIE   How could that even be possible?

RACH   I don't know. But I'm gonna find out.

There's got to be a reason.

...

Four drinks in.

JAMIE   To the best fucking Mayor this town will ever have.

RACH   Fuckin' cheers to that

Jamie?

JAMIE   Yes mate.

RACH   Can I ask you something?

How do you not seem, you know, a mess?

JAMIE   Oh.

RACH   Sorry.
Is that an annoying question? Bringing the mood down.

JAMIE   No. No.

RACH   It must be hard

JAMIE   It is.

RACH   No but it must be. You've been through a lot. I mean.
        Like. A lot.
        More than anyone I've met probably.
        And you seem so.

JAMIE   You know.

RACH   Together.
        No you do. You do. Doesn't he Vin?

        VIN *nods*.

        What was it like being there?

JAMIE   Oh.

RACH   You don't have to talk about it if you don't want to.

JAMIE   No. It's just.
        It's hard.

RACH   Of course.
        Sorry.

        Let's talk about something el–

JAMIE   The green light in the sky.

        That's what I remember.

        The sonic boom.

        The noise of car alarms.

        The sound of panic.

        Dad didn't even put his shoes on. His feet were all
        cut up from the glass. People were in tears, checking
        their phones. All the signal was wiped out. No one
        could tell what was happening.

        We ran. This woman had cut her face. I yanked her
        up, hurt my thumb, calmed her down.

        We could see it was bad. Everyone thought it was a
        nuclear bomb or something.

        I still find it ridiculous. An asteroid.

        It sounds made up.

RACH   That's what I kept saying! Didn't I Vin?

JAMIE   But it's not made up.

RACH   No.

JAMIE   It's not made up and people have died you know my
          mum has died and sometimes I feel like it doesn't
          actually matter that it was an asteroid that killed her
          you know it could have been anything it could have
          been a bus or cancer it's like the actual fact that
          she's dead that is the ridiculous thing. You know
          what I mean?

RACH   I think so.

JAMIE   But then other times I'm like 'an asteroid?'
          Come on.
          You've got to be kidding me.

          When I saw my mum in the hospital... I didn't
          recognise her. Her hair was totally gone.
          Her eyelids too. Her lips. The skin on her face was

          But she looked at me and she recognised me. I could
          see the comfort it gave her. That will stay with me
          forever. I sat with her and gave her water and held her
          hand and she kept doing this thing with her mouth.

          They told me it was a miracle she was alive this long.

          Me and Dad took it in turns to be with her. She died in
          the night as I held her in my arms. I told her I loved
          her. Told her it was okay.

          But in my head I just kept saying.

          Please don't die.
          Please don't die.
          Please don't die.
          I will give anything
          Do anything
          If you just don't die.

          But she did.
          There was nothing I could do to stop her.

RACH   Jesus. Jamie. I'm sorry.

          She puts her hand on his.

JAMIE   You just sort of. Get on with it.

          Vin understands, don't you mate?

          Suddenly VIN *hits himself, open palmed, on the
          head. Slowly at first.*

RACH   Vin?

          Then faster.

          Vin what the fuck –

          Vin.

          Stop it

          Stop it

          *He hits himself and then the table and then himself
          and then the table and then –*

          Fucking stop!

          He stands up.

                              ...

Outside the pub.

RACH   Hey.

          What was that about eh?

          Pretty intense story eh? Why don't you come back
          inside?

          No.

          Okay. Fuck off then.

          He spills his guts in there and you're the one who
          throws a strop? I know you're sad about your dad
          and that but don't you think you've stretched things
          a bit too far? I mean there gets to a point where it's
          just fucking showing off you know it's all a bit look
          at me look how sad I am I've stopped talking
          everybody feel sorry for me.

Look at that guy in there. Look at what he's been
through.

I'm sorry to say it but it's fuckin'

true.

Long silence.

Vin. I'm sorry. I didn't mean that.
I want to have a conversation with you. Don't you
understand that?

Come back inside, eh?

Whatever.

It's cold.

I'm going back in.

                              ...

VIN's house. JAMIE is there.

JAMIE   Rach gave me your address.

          I wanted to say sorry.

          I talk too much. I know that. Always have done.

          I know everybody deals with these things differently.
          And I'm sorry if that story. Upset you. Or.

          She cares about you a lot, Rach.

          You know. There's a part of me that actually enjoys
          telling that story. Getting to the sad parts. Watching
          people's reactions. What's that about?

          Anyway I just wanted to make sure that I hadn't

          VICKY *enters.*

VICKY   Vin?
         Oh hiya.

JAMIE   Hello.

VICKY   I didn't mean to interrupt.

JAMIE   Jamie. Nice to meet you.

VICKY   I'm Vin's mum.
         Vicky.

JAMIE   That is so cool.

VICKY   How do you two know each other?

JAMIE   We're mates.

         I'm staying with Rachel.

VICKY   Rachel?
         Oh is that her name?
         Vin?

         VIN *nods*.

         Well.
         I've heard a lot about Rachel. Apart from her name.
         So thanks for that.

JAMIE   You haven't met?

VICKY   He's been keeping us apart.
         Probably worried what I'll say.

JAMIE   She's an old family friend.
         Been staying with her family since
         I'm from London and my house was destroyed in

VICKY   Oh you're kidding. You were there?

JAMIE   That's right.

VICKY   Oh that's awful.
         And your family?

JAMIE   My mum. She passed.

VICKY   Oh no.

JAMIE   It's been a rough time.

VICKY   I've given to the appeal. Haven't I Vin?
          Donated clothes.

JAMIE   Thank you.
          We appreciate it.

VICKY   If I can ever do anything.

          I love London.
          I do.

          I was so sad to see that happen.

JAMIE   That's very kind.

VICKY   I hope you've got someone looking after you.

JAMIE   I do. Rachel's been so great.
          And Vin, of course.

          You know it's been a real support. Having someone
          who knows a bit about what I'm going through.

VICKY   Right.
          I'm not sure I

JAMIE   With his dad.

          Because they died around the same time.

VICKY   I

          His dad's not dead love.

          He's in Derby.

          Brief silence.

JAMIE   I'm. I'm sorry?

VICKY   He lives in Derby.

          He's not dead. Least as far as I know. He was in
          Corfu last week or so the internet tells me.

          Did he tell you he was dead?

          Brief silence.

JAMIE   No.

           Of course. Sorry.

           I.
           Misspoke.

VICKY   Okay. Because if he's been

JAMIE   No no it's me I misspoke. I got it wrong.
           I was thinking of someone else.

VICKY   Right.

           Okay.

           Well.

           I'll leave you to it.

           Nice to meet you Jamie.

JAMIE   You too.

VICKY   Very sorry for your loss.

           VICKY *leaves*.

           Silence. JAMIE *stares at* VIN.

JAMIE   Mate.

                                 ...

VIN *and* RACH. JAMIE *watches on*.

RACH   Why did you lie?

           I'm gonna ask you again Vin. Why? Actually now
           would be a fucking good time to say something.

           What is wrong with you you fucking freak?
           Seriously?

           SAY SOMETHING.

           VIN *tries to text her*.

           No. No don't text me. Don't fucking

You got something to say to me you can say it.
Out loud.

Oh, what's the point eh? Why bother. Why does
anyone bother trying to make things better why don't
we all just lie down in the muck and let it fucking
wash over us.

They can have this town. Delete it or steal it or
whatever they want. Let it disappear off the map for
all I care. Do you hear me whoever you are? Take it.
Take it all!

I'm done.

STAGE FOUR: DEPRESSION

Estimated death toll: 12,157.

VIN *'s house*. VIN *alone*.

Long silence.

Ages.

•••

VICKY   Gus!
             Gus!
             Gus!
             Gus!
             Gus!
             Dinner!
             Gus!
             Gus!
             Gus!
             Gus!
             Gus!

•••

You haven't seen the cat have you? He's still not back. I know it's silly but. I can't stop picturing him. Lost somewhere.

Or dead. Under the wheels of a car. Or or having crawled under a bush to die. Or with his legs broken. Or his little head squashed.

Silence.

I'm sorry love.

I don't know why I'm crying.

Silly really.

I honestly don't.

•••

VIN *and* VICKY *sit in silence.*

Ages.

...

VIN *in silence.*

Ages.

...

VICKY   One of the neighbours found him.

Hit by a car I think.
He's not breathing, anyway. I know we didn't have him long but

Long silence.

I'm.
I'm struggling a bit love.

I'm not gonna lie.

I don't know why but I'm having a bit of a tough

And it would be nice if
I need a bit of

No. Okay.

Do you know how hard it is?

To have nothing there. Nobody to talk to. To come home and have the house filled with

It's getting to the point where I can't be around you but I'm terrified to leave you alone. I don't know what to do love.

Life's not that easy for any of us. You know that?
There's a big fucking blank space where my life was
supposed to have been and I don't understand how it
got there. But you don't see me moping around like
a fucking mute.

Turn on the news what about them. That friend of
yours. Thousands of lives ruined by chance. But
they're cleaning up. They got on with it. Bit of
character, love, that's all.

Please. Talk to me.
Say something.
Anything.
One word

A noise even.

Just. Something.

Say something.

Say something.

Say something. Say something. Say something.
Say something. Say something. Say something.
Say something. Say something. Say something
say something say something say something say
something say something say something I can't do
this any more can't talk to myself any more I'm
going crazy I'm going fucking crazy.

I can't take

This

Silence.

I'm sorry.

I need you to

I need

...

RACH*'s driveway.*

RACH   Go home Vin. You can't just wait in my driveway.
        Mum told you already.

        What you did is actually a pretty fucked-up thing to do
        to another person. Do you understand that? Especially
        the only one who gives you the time of day.

        I mean. We had a fucking funeral. It'd be funny if it
        wasn't so

        You must've known I would find out eventually.
        What was your long-term plan?

        Don't you understand you idiot?

        I liked you.
        A lot.
        More than that even.

        But I can't be your friend unless you're honest
        with me.

        I can't help you if you don't tell me what's going on.
        Nobody can.

        She waits for a response.

        No?

        Then go home Vin. Please. And leave me alone.

        Because it's fucking exhausting.

        VIN *watches her leave.*

        VIN *tries to speak.*

*He's furious. Wants to hit something. Or someone.
There's nothing to hit.*

The anger builds

Tries to scream

He can't

The anger builds

Tries to scream

He can't

The anger builds and builds and builds and he

Explodes

*Furious with himself. With his throat his larynx his
vocal chords. His tongue.*

He tears at himself.

Hurts himself.

*Tearing and hurting again and again smacking
whatever is near to him his body the floor his body
the floor then himself and then the floor and then
himself and then the floor again and again punching
his way to the core of the Earth the anger pouring
out of every part of him until – until –*

JAMIE   Vin?

JAMIE *is stood there in the driveway of the house he
is staying in, holding a blue carrier bag.*

VIN *looks at him.*

What you

What you doing?

I just bought some cans.

Fancy one?

I could

I could really use a drink.

...

The two young men drink their cans.

JAMIE   Just spoke to my dad.
I'm going back to London.

My house has been declared safe. So that's. A relief.

Can't wait to get home. Cannot wait.

Cheers.

Brief silence.

Sorry I grassed you up.

Rachel still pissed?

VIN *looks at him.*

Yeah.

Although I'm not sure beating yourself up in her driveway is the best way to

Fair enough.

I just. Don't understand why you would lie about something that big.

Silence.

You know what. That's not true.

My mum. She didn't die in my arms. I told you she did but

I mean I was there. In the burns unit. And I saw her saw all her. Skin and that.

But I got to the door of her room and I could hear her

calling for me and I couldn't go in. And I turned to go and my dad grabbed my hand but I wrenched it away and I left the hospital.

I went and got chips and by the time I came back she had died.

I dislocated my thumb. I wrenched my hand away so hard that I dislocated my thumb. I don't know why I lied about that.

Silence. JAMIE *wipes his eyes.*

State of the two of us eh? Jesus.

VIN *puts his hand on* JAMIE*'s shoulder.*

Cheers.

…

VIN*'s house.* RACH *and* VICKY. VICKY *is holding a cat basket.*

VICKY   So you're Rachel.

RACH   That's right.

VICKY   Rachel from the pub.

RACH   I guess so.

VICKY   Thanks for coming.

RACH   When I got your text –

VICKY   He's upstairs.

            Silence.

RACH   What's in the

VICKY   A cat.

RACH   Aw!

VICKY   He's dead.

RACH   Oh.

VICKY   I'm going to bury him in the garden.

It's nice.
Finally meeting you.

RACH   You too.

VICKY   Can I
Does he. Does he talk to you?

RACH   Nah.

VICKY   Okay. That's what I thought.

RACH   Can I ask.
And tell me if it's none of my business because it's
usually not. But.
What caused it?

VICKY   I'm sorry

RACH   The reason why he can't speak.
I thought it was. Something else.

But it's not that.
So I was

Was it to do with London?
When he heard the news maybe?

VICKY   I don't think so.
It's started about a week before.

RACH   Oh.

VICKY   This is the longest it's ever lasted.

RACH   It's happened before?

VICKY   He didn't tell you?

When he was younger.
I would notice him talking less and less.
The words would drain away until
And then one day they'd be back.
It hasn't happened for years. I thought he'd grown
out of it.

This time's different. I don't know.

He refuses to get help and I don't know what else I can

I can't force him. You know?

VIN *enters. Stares at them.*

RACH   Hiya Vin.

I'm at your house.

Brief silence.

VICKY   Well.

I better get on. This hole won't dig itself.

Nice to meet you Rach.

RACH   Sorry about your cat.

VICKY   It's alright.
He wasn't really ours.
Just a visitor really.

VICKY *leaves.*

RACH   I wasn't gonna come but.
Jamie convinced me.

Still not texting me. Okay.

You don't make it easy, do you mate?

Silence.

I've been thinking a lot about why you'd lie to me
like that. Why anyone would lie about something
like that when there are so many people going
through terrible shit for real. And I was so angry with
you. I'm still fucking angry with you.

But I think part of it. At least. Is on me.

I came round here to get you to tell me the truth. The
real truth. I've always thought I could help you if I
could find what was wrong.

But it's not as simple as that. Is it?

Look at me. Whatever's going on in there. However big or small or stupid you might think it is. You don't have to justify it. To me. Or to anyone.

If you're feeling it.

Then it's real. Okay?

Because there are people who will help you. You've only got to ask.

She waits for him to answer. Silence. Ages.

You know. Things are still going missing.

The other day I was in town and there was just this hole where a pavement slab should be. It wasn't dug up, there wasn't building works going on. All the other slabs were perfectly normal but where this one was was just this, deep, black hole. I stood there ages, kept waiting for someone to fall in, but they never did.

I'll see you Vin.

RACH *leaves.*

VIN *alone for a while.*

Silence.

VICKY *returns.*

VICKY   The strangest thing just happened. I'd finished digging the hole and I reached into the basket to take him out. And I lay him on the grass and thought. I'll give him a stroke just to say goodbye. Say some words.

And so I'm crying and I'm stroking him and I'm saying some words and then all of a sudden

He purred.

He purred and his tail started moving. And he got up. And he looked at me. And he walked away and climbed over the fence.

I don't know if he wasn't dead. Or he was dead and now he's not.

I wonder if that's ever happened before.

Seems

impossible.

Suddenly VIN *tries something. He hums, feeling the voice in the back of his throat.*

VIN   Mm

Mmmm

It is the first noise she's heard him make in months.

VICKY   Vin?

VIN   Mmmm

VICKY   What you

VIN   Mmmmmmmmmmmmmmmmmmmmmmmmm
Mmmmmmmmmmmmmmmmmmmmmmmmm
Mmmmmmmmmmmmmmmmmmmmmmmmmmmmmmmm
mmmmmmmmmmmmmmmm

VIN suddenly breaks down crying. He cries into his mother's arms. He cries and he cries and he cries.

VICKY   Hey. It's alright baby.
It's alright.
I got you.

Your mum's got you.

...

VICKY   I'm sorry I lost my temper the other day.
          I know it's not your fault.

          I just want you to be
          Us to be

          You know what?

          Neither of us are doing that well, are we?

VIN   **Mum.**

VICKY   Oh.
          You text me. You feel okay texting me?

          She beams.

          Well. That's. Okay.

VIN   **I need help.**

VICKY   What can I

VIN   **If I keep on like this I'm gonna**

          explode.

VICKY   Hey.
          It's alright.
          We'll sort something.

          Don't want you exploding eh? You'd wreck my carpet.

          Whatever help you need, we'll get it.
          I promise.

STAGE FIVE: ACCEPTANCE

Time since impact: 367 days 5 hours 4 minutes 11 seconds.

VIN *and* RACH.

RACH   Vin.

Hiya. Thought that was you.

Been ages. How you doing?

Still not talking?

VIN   **Same number?**

RACH   Same number yeah.

VIN   **It's good to see you.**

RACH   You too.

Brief silence.

VIN   **What's new?**

RACH   Quit the call centre.

Looking at doing social work maybe. Think that might be alright.
Can't fix everything. But I can do a bit, you know?

Still time to be Mayor one day.

VIN   **Get Jamie to write a campaign song.**

RACH   Oh god.

He's back with his dad.
Keeps inviting me to stay with him but. I don't really fancy it.

VIN   **I'd like to see the crater.**

RACH   They've already started building on it.

Can't believe it's been a year.

It was the maddest thing and now it's just something that happened, you know what I mean?

VIN   **Rach.**

            I'm sorry.

RACH   Shut up.

VIN   **You were a good mate. And I lied to you.**

RACH   It was ages ago.
           How's it all going?

VIN   **Better.**

RACH   That's good.

           He puts his index finger up as if to say 'hang on'.

           He signs something in BSL.

           Shit. Is that real?
           What did it say?

VIN   **'Rachel for Mayor.'**

RACH   Amazing.

VIN   **I think.**
            Not very good yet.

RACH   You got some help?
           That's great Vin. That's really great.

           Brief silence.

           Did you see?
           Couldn't fucking believe it.
           Swimming pool's back. Slide and everything.
           Maybe they were only borrowing it.

VIN   **There's something I should say.**

           VIN *tries to speak. Takes a while. Struggles. Keeps trying.*

RACH   It's alright.

           I know.

           You don't have to.

           I should get off. I'm meeting

It's been good to see you mate. You look after yourself, okay?

He nods. She hugs him, and turns to walk away. And then suddenly three words from deep inside VIN *rise to the top and erupt into the air between them.*

VIN   Thank.

          You.

                    Rach.

She turns back.

He seems surprised by his own voice. He tries it again. Once more, more confidently this time, from the bottom of his heart.

The two friends smile at each other.

Thank you.

Other Titles in this Series

A Nick Hern Book

Lava first published in Great Britain as a paperback original in 2018 by
Nick Hern Books Limited, The Glasshouse, 49a Goldhawk Road, London
W12 8QP, in association with Fifth Word

This revised edition first published in 2022

Designed and typeset by Nick Hern Books, London
Printed in Great Britain by Mimeo Ltd, Huntingdon, Cambridgeshire PE29 6XX

A CIP catalogue record for this book is available from the British Library

ISBN 978 1 83904 098 6

www.nickhernbooks.co.uk

facebook.com/nickhernbooks

twitter.com/nickhernbooks